# The Pretty Thoughts of a Hot Chick!

## Foxy Little Notions for Our Minds, Bodies and Souls!

### By Alicia Marie Rivers

Book jacket design:
Randell Pearson, rpeardesign@aol.com
Photo: Fred Sly, www.fslyphotography.com
Makeup: Kim W., www.modelmayhem.com/artistaq

iUniverse, Inc.
New York   Bloomington

**The Pretty Thoughts of a Hot Chick!**
**Foxy Little Notions for Our Minds, Bodies, and Souls!**

*iUniverse books may be ordered through booksellers or by contacting:*

*iUniverse*
*1663 Liberty Drive*
*Bloomington, IN 47403*
*www.iuniverse.com*
*1-800-Authors (1-800-288-4677)*

*ISBN: 978-1-4401-1261-4 (sc)*
*ISBN: 978-1-4401-1262-1 (ebook)*

*Printed in the United States of America*

*iUniverse rev. date: 1/26/2009*

*This book is dedicated to women who've been hurt and lost their footing…*

*"Your happiness begins and ends with your thoughts..."*

# Preface

At times, we lose ourselves in our dreams, insecurities, fears, career, family, affairs and hardships forsaking our true passions and identities to appease a single mood, entity, perception or reason. I was inspired to write this book because I was once in a dark place that nearly swallowed my joy and almost cost me my most prized jewels...my self-love and peace of mind. But, due to my pretty thoughts born out of a few hard lessons, I rescued me...

*A Hot Chick is unapologetically confident… unapologetically sexy and smart… unapologetically feminine…unapologetically playful, strong, experienced & fearless…the Hot Chick is you (even if you have yet to meet her or have not been formally introduced)!*

# Table of Contents

**Introduction** ............................................. xv

**1 - How to think like a Hot Chick!** ........................... 1

**2 - I believe in my beauty...** ...........................4
You are as you think you are...

**3 - I own my worth!** .................................. 17
Be your lover for life...

**4 - Men and me.** .................................44
Guys are like shoes....

**5 - The art of my feminine allure...** .......................70
A truly self-assured *Hot Chick* has oodles of
body pride...

**6 – Affairs of my heart** ...............................84
More often than not, we seek our happiness
from other people instead of ourselves...

**7 – Live Pretty!** .....................................112
Let what pleasures you be your guide...

**8 - Let that be the reason** ............................. 124
3 things in life that once gone, never come
back: time, words & opportunity...

**9 – An AfterThought** .............................154

**Acknowledgments** ...............................171

# Introduction

Most of us feel pretty good with ourselves, right? Wrong! Think about it. Are you constantly filled with thoughts of self-doubt? Do you second-guess your appeal? Are you avoiding seeing yourself in a mirror for fear of what you think others perceive? Do you agonize over your physical attributes, i.e. weight, teeth, complexion, breast size, butt size, hair texture, hair length, etc? Are you secretly worried that you are not good enough for anyone or anything? Are you in a relationship that is no longer working and haven't found the strength to leave? Do you feel that you're in a dead-in job with no hopes of a future? Are you in love with someone who does not give a damn about you? Do you feel like giving up on your dreams? Or, do you simply need a boost every now and then? Girl, I know just how you feel!

I went from a great job, no financial worries, a cute apartment, a passionate relationship and starting my own magazine (with wonderful success moments) to a company in turmoil, frustration with my business partners, no money, the possibility of losing my dream as well as coming to terms with the end of a tumultuous love affair and leaving my home. I was devastated. I had no where to turn or so I thought.

Life is a trip and a half, honey! But, I am a living testimony of how pretty thoughts changed my circumstance. After many months of drowning with the weight of a bruised and confused heart, a dream deferred and a spirit defeated, I fell into a deep depression where nothing mattered except my hurt, TV, a few glasses of wine or a beer, the passing company of men and the lie I told myself daily that I was okay. I was not. My self-esteem and focus had faltered. However, one day I stumbled across an idea I wrote, promoted and believed in: *"You are who you think you are!"* Upon seeing this, a light bulb went off in my head and a tidal wave of emotions cleansed my soul for what seemed like days. It was the wake-up call I needed to remind me that just because I got knocked down, does not mean that I stay down.

So girl, after many moons of being at my lowest point, I formed one hell of a threesome…*me, myself and I*…loved myself more and got down to business! This included learning to forgive people, but more importantly I forgave myself because I had to accept responsibility for the mistakes I made. Plus, I realized that people do according to their understanding and I finally understood that no one is responsible for my happiness, livelihood or safe haven except me. Thus, I became not only or even a survivor…but a **Hot Chick**!

Today, as I achieve one goal after another, hit hurdles, face truths and fears, one thing is certain…I choose to smile, laugh and live pretty instead of letting disappointments control my thoughts then devour my spirit where bitterness can breed and rob me of my joy. Yes, I know…easier said than done, right?

Picture this for a moment. When you agonize over a particular person, thing or situation, such as doubt, lack of funds, what you do not have, other people's opinions, how people have treated you, etc., it consumes you and becomes all that you think about…all that you see… all that you are. For example, if you think you're broke then you'll always be broke. If you feel that you're not worthy, then you won't be. If you believe men are no good, then they'll never be. Simply put, you and your condition become…your reality. You see darling, by giving something so much attention and thinking negatively, you create a beast and give it the fuel it needs to destroy your confidence, purpose and glee. Hey, life will always present us with a twist or two. Yet, with belief and strength, a **Hot Chick** can get through anything!

Now, what are you prepared to think and do?

# 1 - How to think like a Hot Chick!

Hot chicks are not born, they're created! They nurture their special brand of hotness and do not allow negativity; low self-esteem, and/or someone's opinion take up valuable space in their minds. Why? Because that's what they CHOOSE, darling! Hot chicks are focused on their happiness. They live as they believe and there is no difference between what they think and do. So if you want to be desirable and irresistible or you yearn for something better or different, start with what you think; which leads to your action then becomes your lifestyle. Hence, take a deep breath and contemplate yourself in the image you want to exude and inhabit the following beliefs:

1. *My beauty, including intelligence & common sense, is a conscious choice and a daily practice.*

2. *I may get bruised, but I'm never broken!*

3. *Style is how I decide to speak to the world.*

4. *I have the power to manifest my desires through pretty thoughts, visualization, dedication, persistence, intention and action!*

5. *I live in the moment and appreciate the journey.*

6. *Great sex starts with me.*

7. *A good cry is essential, but a smile is an every day rule!*

8. *I am never afraid to find the humor in my mistakes and embarrassing moments.*

9. *Sex appeal is more than physical attractiveness. It is my body language - how I feel, speak, walk, sit, stand, gesture and move.*

Now that you've got the principles, welcome to the mind of the hot chick!

## 2 - I believe in my beauty

You are who you think you are. Live it! Breathe it! Perception is reality. Beauty is in the eye of the beholder and you are the most important observer. Remember, beauty is a state of mind and if you believe it, you will achieve it!

"Pretty women wonder where my secret lies…"
-Maya Angelou, "Phenomenal Women"
from AND STILL I RISE

### *Pretty is as pretty does…*

*I was not always so sure of my beauty. Many moons ago, I would give too much power to the notion that a beautiful, sexy woman couldn't have flaws…that she had to fit a certain make, model or mode. But one day, after yet another crying fit over what I did not have, or a new bump or two, I realized after seeing my reflection through tear-stained eyes that I was whatever I chose to be. You see, beauty is an aesthetic comprehension, which is purely subjective. It is an idea…most notably a belief…of being a woman who knows who she is and how she chooses to be pretty to the world. Just because you're not thin, don't have a big butt, certain facial features, big boobs, small boobs, long hair, a particular hair texture, perfect skin or you're a little older than the rest, doesn't mean that you can't be just as hot as the next woman. Hey, beauty is like ice cream—there are many delicious flavors enjoying their rightful place on this smorgasbord of prettiness. So why not embrace your particular brand of allure? You've got to believe it in order to achieve it honey, and if you do, others will follow. So, go ahead and carry yourself like a beautiful woman. Remember, how the world responds to you is up to you! It is by your thoughts, hand and command!*

*The notion, "If I lost 10 more pounds then I would be…" or "I hate my…" stops immediately because what I focus on the most becomes my reality. For example, if I only think and complain about how much I hate what I believe to be a certain flaw then I will attract people who will see my perceived flaw. But, if I keep my mouth closed and my thoughts focused on my favorite attributes, then my insecurities will diminish and I as well as others will see my beauty.*

*I am not allowing other people's
criticisms or opinions of me set the
standard for whom or what I am.*

*I am proud to be me.*

*Every day I choose something in my
life and/or about myself that I feel good
about and immerse myself in it.*

*One of the secrets of confidence is utilizing perception to define a reality that people operate in as if it were their own belief.*

*Another pimple! Oh well…good morning darling. But damn, I still look good!*

*I will not think negatively! I do not believe in my last thought. I am starting over. I am thinking something pretty right now.*

*The greatest trick many men and women
have ever pulled was convincing me that I
was not worthy and that my beauty
did not exist.*

*Look at yourself in the mirror and repeat...* "There is not a single day that goes by that I do not love you more."

*Whatever I focus on the most…*
*negative situation, comments or*
*people, becomes my truth.*

*Damn, I cannot fit this…oh well…*
*never I mind. I have something*
*else that will look just as hot!*

# 3 - I own my worth!

Be your lover for life! Create a never-ending romance with yourself by caring and nurturing your mind, body and spirit. For example, write yourself a love letter or poem, treat yourself to an exotic getaway or buy yourself flowers once or twice a week. When you know your value and pamper yourself, the very essence of who you are is strengthened, fulfilled and powerful.

"Sow a thought, and you reap an act; Sow an act, and you reap a habit; Sow a habit, and you reap a character; Sow a character, and you reap a destiny."
-Charles Read

*Why do we feel the need to be validated by others?*

*For some intangible reason other than what we have been conditioned to believe, we have always sought a confirmation on our intelligence, talents, attractiveness, style, a person's attitude toward us, etc. Maybe it dates back to our childhood - the absence or neglect of a father, emotional abuse from a mother, peer pressure or simply our innate sensibilities. Perhaps it's a combination of things. Whatever the case, we should not give a damn! We don't need anybody to authenticate our value. We put far too much emphasis on folk's opinions, too much time and thought into their judgments (that includes those of family, friends, lovers, co-workers, strangers as well as members of our church, sorority, etc.) Of course, we all want to be accepted, but it should never be at your expense...or better yet the cost of depreciating your worth! Simply put, you are exactly as YOU believe. So, don't think you are. Know you are!*

*Without self respect, I have no sense of*
*who I am or what I can achieve....*

*If I want to be treasured, I must first believe in my worth and treasure myself.*

*I am not afraid to stand alone.*
*I trust me.*

*Winning is also getting up after I've fallen when no one else thought I could or should!*

*Isn't it interesting how someone's disapproval
can send me into negativity
and self-doubt?*

*Other people's opinions have no real lasting impact – whether it's positive or negative - except for the value I place on it!*

*I never settle for less than I rightfully deserve.*

*Life is a banquet and most of us are starving to death. I choose to eat heartily.*

*The only thing constant in life is change.*
*So I am ready when it comes knocking.*

*My love for me is too much to accept anyone's bullshit.*

*I will starve if I eat all the lies people feed me. So, I listen to my intuition and I don't go hungry.*

*I will not let my fears prevent me from reaching my personal best.*

*What makes people take risks, go the
extra mile and do whatever it takes
to achieve their goals?. . .Passion.*

*I have the power to create the existence I want.*

*I will not compromise my values. It is my belief that I can live my best life now!*

*As worried and/or fearful as I may be,*
*I will do it anyway!*

*Anything is possible, regardless of
my situation right this moment.*

*My life is guided by my thoughts and
whatever I focus on expands.*

*I walk as though the world is at my
feet, in my hands and between my ears,
arms and thighs…because it is.*

*I never apologize for pursuing what makes me happy.*

*Just because he or she is unable to see my worth & beauty does not mean it doesn't exist.*

*Pure joy and freedom begins with the thought of self-love complemented by the act.*

*The gravity of my problems is never the issue. It is not what happens to me that will determine my outcome; it is how I handle and roll with it.*

*I will never take a "no" to mean that I cannot do a certain something to fulfill my hopes and dreams. I just have to find another route.*

*If I do not think for myself, then someone else will do the thinking for me.*

# 4 - Men and me.

*Men are like shoes. Some look good but just don't feel right. Some feel better after you try them on for size. And some are best right where you found them.*

**"*The aim in life is self-development, to realize one's nature perfectly.*"**
–Oscar Wilde

*Why do we seem to miss what we think we once had?*

*Think about it? When we start dating "Mr. Wonderful" everything is terrific. He's showering you with affection, special little gifts and he's doing his best to increase your happiness. You have this air of mystery as you still hang out with your friends; spend time with yourself– all while treating him good, one spoonful at a time. Now as the relationship matures, you replace that spoon with a dump truck, giving him more attention, neglecting your old activities and losing yourself completely in him. Then, he starts to become a bit distant. Those times and tokens of adoration begin to subside and you're left wondering, "what happened?" He starts to treat you like the 'old ball and chain', expecting more yet doing less. But let's not get this twisted. This is not about him. It's about you! It always has been. You see, we have to maintain our sense of self and refrain from getting caught up in pleasing him. Simply put, do not live for or because of him. Live for you! Your happiness comes from what's inside you. Contrary to popular belief, it is not because of how, what or who he is nor with what he has done for you. You know what you bring to the table, honey! Believe in your allure! Remember, as long as you're doing things that make you feel good, like nourishing your mind and spirit, maintaining your appearance and staying focused on your personal and professional goals, then and only then will you never miss what you thought you once had.*

*Embrace being single and see each guy you meet as an option, not a goal.*

*Unless I take ownership of my value,
I'll forever be needy and desperate in
my selection of friends and lovers.*

*Before I give him another chance or give myself to yet another lover, I will ask myself...is it just the lonely talking again?*

*I am not worried about what he is doing or with what he may or will do. I am only focused on what I'm doing right now.*

*I combine the lady and the vamp.
It is far more intriguing and
mystifying when both co-exist.*

*I can have any man I choose as
long as I believe it to be true.*

*Although I still love him . . .
I love me more.*

*If I looked in a mirror and saw myself as hot & precious, I would not turn to men or food because I am all the comfort I need.*

*As I joyfully gaze upon my reflection, I smile right back at me. But, sometimes as I openly grin at my mirror image he winks back just over my shoulder…and he is <u>only</u> the cherry on top of this delicious sundae!*

*Flirt with a handsome stranger. Give him a wink and a smile. Then go on about your business.*

*Lick the ice cream off his fingers
instead of yours.*

*I am not waiting by the phone to hear from him. I have more important things to do.*

*When a man buys me a drink, it is perceived as an investment of things to come. But, when I decline or buy a man a drink, it keeps it on a fair exchange level.*

*I don't need to keep talking endlessly to express myself. Silence speaks volumes.*

*I do not apologize for setting standards. I know what I can work with and what I cannot tolerate.*

*I am not allowing the depth of my
love for him diminish my dignity.*

*Love is blind & what feels good isn't always right for me! So I never lose sight of my three best friends - me, myself & I.*

*One of the best lessons I've learned from my ex is that what was once a boy does not necessarily become a man. Age is <u>not</u> synonymous with maturity or wisdom.*

*A man's love is not determined solely by what he pays for, the laundry he does or the number of times he cooks or cleans, but by how he treats you, whether he truly listens to you as well as how he speaks to and of you especially when he is angry, justified or not.*

*I will never allow my love for a man
to outweigh my love for self!*

*An unrequited love is like a moth to a flame burned by desire and because it makes me miserable, I will free myself and blow it out.*

*Invite him to taste your drink or food but....off the tip of your finger.*

*As the storm clears and the anger lessens,*
*my mind will warn me to let him go*
*as my body yearns for his touch. But,*
*my spirit will whisper "lesson learned"*
*as I close my eyes and finally let go.*

*I am not picking up the phone when he calls this time, because I am unavailable. I will return his call later or in a day or so.*

# 5 - The art of my feminine allure

A truly self-assured *Hot Chick* has oodles of body pride and is never shy about highlighting her assets! Beauties, by showing off your best qualities, it helps shape the way you see yourself.

"You don't move just because you want to go from this point to that point - the body has to be using the words as well as you vocally use the words."
- Eartha Kitt

*Ladies, a woman's middle name should be sensuality. Hey, it is an important part of who you are. By the way, that is the secret of some of the world's sexiest women! So embrace the sexual and sensual aspect of your being darling. Here's how!*

1. *Every chance you get lovingly caress that hot body of yours because you must know pleasure to give it.*

2. *Dance seductively to your favorite song as you get dressed or undressed. (See the \*Hot Chick Play List below for ideas.)*

3. *Visualize yourself taking control. Imagine making the first move, stealing the first kiss, or whispering your intentions into the ear of your lover as you softly run your fingers down or up his arm, across his knee or down the back of his neck. Then, wink and tell him "good night" or "until we meet again."*

4. *Focus on your positives. Don't sell yourself short because you are not perfect. You are hot despite your perceived imperfections. Losing your fears and inhibitions requires loving yourself completely and stretching out of your comfort zone in order to be a hottie!*

5. *At least one day a week, take a candlelight bubble bath filled with rose petals and a pinch of*

      *sandalwood, Egyptian musk or amber oil, while sipping a glass of wine.*

6. *Never leave the house without mascara, lip-gloss and of course wearing your sexiest bra and panties...even the cute cotton ones! Golden rule: A woman looks and feels good for her first.*

7. *Commit the following to memory from the late screen actress, Mae West:*

"I speak two languages, Body and English."

\*The *Hot Chick* Playlist:

1. *Rope Burn – Janet Jackson*
2. *Come and Talk to Me – Jodeci*
3. *Say Yes – Floetry*
4. *No Ordinary Love - Sade*
5. *Rock the Boat – Aaliyah*
6. *Anytime, Anyplace – Janet Jackson*
7. *Til the Cops Come Knocking – Maxwell*
8. *Slow Love – Prince*
9. *Let's Get it On – Marvin Gaye*
10. *Strawberry Bounce – Janet Jackson*
11. *Wifey - Next*
12. *The Most Beautiful Girl in the World – Prince*
13. *Nasty Girl – Vanity 6*
14. *Lay Down – Floetry*
15. *Don't Cha – Pussycat Dolls*
16. *Superwoman – Alicia Keys*
17. *Beauty – Dru Hill*
18. *Come Inside - Intro*

*Of all the things to wear to enhance my beauty, confidence is the most striking.*

*It isn't the eyes, lips, hair or body that is so beautiful. I just know how to use them.*

*I will drown out my stresses while I frolic
in a scented bubble bath with a pinch of
vanilla and cinnamon essential oils, a touch
of honey and a dash of milk, as I sip a glass
of champagne and make exquisite love
to my deserving body.*

*I am slipping into my best dress or
outfit and admiring the view.*

*Good posture with a hip swaying stride is one of the ultimate forms of body language that communicates feminine allure.*

*I welcome every inch of me.*

*I do not underestimate the power of my womanly appeal.*

*Living pretty is not just a lipstick, great hairstyle, hot shoes and clothes but the belief that I can be, do and have anything.*

*The true meaning of sensual pleasure can only be found when I look in the mirror and enjoy every morsel of me.*

*Being a knockout is not about the way I look. It is the way I am.*

# 6  Affairs of my heart

Over and over again, we expect our happiness to come from other people instead of ourselves...

"Mistakes are the portals of discovery."
- James Joyce

# *What lessons have you learned from your relationships?*

*Each person and every situation that has come into your life has taught you something. And whether the lesson was hard fought, painful or pleasant, it guided you to the next encounter in either a positive or negative way. But ladies, remember this (and you might not agree with me now and I certainly did not believe this sometime ago), there really is no such thing as a failed relationship, wasted time or quite frankly being a fool. Look at it this way. You had the faith to experiment. Now you can take the knowledge, be a better person as a result of it and move on to greater things.*

*Without integrity, there is no love;
without trust, there is no peace; without
confidence there is no beauty.*

*Music ties my passion and pain, tap dances on my heart and stirs my soul.*

*To listen well, I must discern between my truth and the truth being told to me. My truth is not everyone's reality.*

*Sometimes I have to walk away from someone or things I love or step outside my comfort zone to save my most vital love…me.*

*No matter how upset he or she may get, they'll be alright!*

*People often tell me who they are. So it is up to me to stop hearing what I want to hear & start heeding THEIR words & actions!*

*Regardless of the type of relationship I'm in, I am always in control of my emotions and thus my reactions.*

*Forgiveness is freeing! It is something I do for myself. It doesn't mean the other person was correct in their actions that hurt me. It is simply my willingness to understand and let go.*

*It is pointless and stressful to argue
with another person's truth or belief.*

*Every friendly face, every nice gesture, every passionate embrace is not meant to remain forever.*

*What someone assumes has no bearing on me, because if I don't mind, it does not matter!*

*I will not continue to hurt myself
to maintain a toxic relationship
or keep a situation in tact.*

*More often than not, people cannot see past their own feelings, experiences and desires.*

*I am choosing my friends, lovers and business associates wisely, because I am the company I keep!*

*I will not allow my emotions to cloud my ability to think clearly.*

*The biggest misstep we make in any relationship is not seeing ourselves as the prize.*

*I must be honest with who I am first, before I decide who or how someone else should be.*

*Slow down darling. Take a moment and be still. Chaos is never good for my mind, body or spirit.*

*Sometimes its best to "keep it in my pocket", or sit on information until I can come from a position of strength before confronting the intended.*

*I will not win by telling the truth and I will not lose by hearing it. The truth is the strongest game in the world.*

*When truly loved there is a warmth
and tenderness that shines from the eyes
and smile and rests upon the soul.*

*Being happy doesn't mean everything's perfect. It just means I've decided to see beyond the imperfections.*

*Paying attention only costs
me a little patience.*

*If a person cannot accept responsibility
for his/her actions, let 'em go!*

*Not everyone or every situation is at it seems.*

*Sometimes the prize is not worth the pain. So it is up to me to decide when to leave well enough alone.*

# 7 Live Pretty!

Let what pleasures you be your guide...

"I have no regrets. Regrets only make wrinkles."
- Sophia Loren

*Remember the last time you were in ecstasy? Whether it was during a delicious meal, relaxing bath, glorious massage, great movie or show, delightful get-a-way, long walk, good read, pleasant memories or steamy sex, your attention was on the physical and mental bliss. So, when you concentrate on what makes you feel good through sight, touch, taste, smell and sound, you tune into your pleasure zone and release anything that displeases you. This causes a euphoric state of mind that leads to a mood of complete satisfaction. Even small things like laughter, regular manicures and pedicures, getting your hair tended to, spraying on your favorite fragrance or slipping on a scented body lotion, amps up your gratification level.*

*Life isn't so tough. It is how we choose to live that makes it hard.*

*An absence of passion is an absence of life itself.*

*I am worth more to myself and the world when I am pleasured.*

*Pleasure is the guiding principle in
my life to live my best life now.*

*I am never embarrassed to let my true feelings show, too proud to laugh at my own silly mistakes or too mature to get a little silly.*

*I do not apologize for spoiling myself!*

*Self satisfaction and frequent orgasms adds to my glow! So I am quite acquainted with Bobby (my boobs), Thomas (my thighs), Bill (my butt) and Vincent (my vagina) and often include their friends Victor (my vibrator) and Frank (my fingers) for pure rapture.*

*I will take a moment and quiet my mind.*

*I am the only love that can light my life
and make things right.*

*Laughter is truly life's best medicine.*

## 8 - Let that be the reason

Three things in life that once gone, never come back: time, words & opportunity…

*"The first recipe for happiness is to avoid
lengthy meditations on the past."*
- Andre Maurois

*When will I stop crying for the little girl in me?*

*He was a pretty powerful figure in my life for several years.
He was handsome, strong, charming, charismatic, a talented
singer as well as…absent, selfish, arrogant and cruel. I adored
and feared him. I wanted to be every beautiful thing he saw
in himself and in me. But he physically and mentally abused
every woman who ever attempted to love him…nameless
faces in a turbulent sea of sex and violence. One evening, he
finally gave me a taste of his poison. And as he stood within
inches of my lips, with images of a woman's blood-spattered
face dancing in my head, my innocence disappeared…*

*A few years later after taking a real hard look at myself and
the cocky men I was subsequently attracted to, I realized
that in order to experience peace and real happiness, I must
learn to forgive and walk away feeling good with me. You
know, I ran into that "pretty powerful figure" right after
my self-analysis and healing and agreed to have lunch with
him. But, by the end of his explanation for his past behavior
and abandonment, I gathered my things, touched his hand
and said, "I forgive you…Goodbye Daddy."*

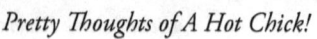
*When you stop looking, you start living.*

*If I take responsibility, I can effect change.*
*If I don't, I'll always be a victim.*

*Sometimes we remain in situations longer than we should. Simply put, one of the saddest things in life is wondering "what if…"*

*When I am focused it is impossible
to throw me off my course.*

*Don't worry about it baby, this too shall pass!*

*It is not just the words one speaks that should provoke a response, but the meaning within the words & actions as well as what one does not do that should arouse curiosity.*

*Putting down another woman's appearance may make you feel temporarily superior, but in actuality you're more likely to see imperfections in yourself. Not to mention, you'd look catty and unconfident. Instead, praise your positive traits as well as those of other women.*

*My appearance affects people's perception
of me, i.e., financial status, character,
intelligence, authority, strength,
confidence, trustworthiness as well
as their behavior towards me.*

*People do according to their understanding.*

*Failure doesn't mean that I cannot attain success. It just means that I have to go about it in a different way.*

*To forgive is to set the prisoner free and
finally discover that the prisoner was me.*

*The words "can't," "won't," and "shouldn't,"*
*no longer exist in my vocabulary.*

*Obsessing and worrying about a situation ignites stress & frustration. I will replace with a calm assurance & attract a desired solution.*

*When we lose people or things it is simply
a reminder to cherish what we have now.*

*I choose to feel good everyday. Happiness is a choice, just as anger, sadness or envy.*

*Words help define who we are and most of us don't truly understand the words we speak.*

*Release the pain & bitterness. In order to heal I must learn to forgive. So I choose to live! Because whatever I sow, my spirit will reap.*

*Good byes are tough, especially to a love affair or dream. But, it is soothing to my mind and soul when I gather my strength and move on.*

*My life is not determined by what happens to me but by the attitude I bring to life.*

*I will not focus on the past. The chapter is closed! I am concentrating on what I have now.*

*Everything's alright when I smile.*

*I acknowledge and give thanks
for all that I have and want.*

*I am no longer imprisoned by past disappointments and hurt.*

*A rude remark, low funds, a bad hair day, a few extra pounds or a pimple does not mean the end of the world.*

*No one can ever come between me
and my happiness except me.*

*If I do not stay informed about my business or my job, I will increase my chances of missing great opportunities.*

*When or if I fall, feel lost or low, I will rise as the sun shines again.*

*Positive feelings help me thrive, but
pretty thoughts keep my energy alive.*

# 9 An AfterThought

I once found myself in the midst of a very bad breakup that left me pretty wounded. It is difficult when you think your man is your best friend then come to the startling realization that he is not the man you romanticized in your mind. Love can make us blind ladies or honestly speaking, the need to be loved. For me, it was a crippling desire to be comforted emotionally after years of feeling abandoned by my first love as well as after a long day of dealing within an industry that is shameless in its biases and feeds on your talent yet preys on your weaknesses. But at the end of the day, it is up to you to accept it or not.

"You're alive. Do something. The directive in life, the moral imperative was so uncomplicated. It could be expressed in single words, not complete sentences. It sounded like this: Look. Listen. Choose. Act."
- Barbara Hall

*What steps are you taking on your journey to true happiness?*

*Have you ever been in bed with someone and felt lonelier than when no one lay beside you? Are you still waiting for a prince to awaken your sleeping beauty? Do you regret a few decisions you made in life, career and love? Well, here's the real kicker…this is by your choice and honey we are the choices we do and do not make. You see, life teaches us many lessons. Some we pass. Others we fail to learn. And a few we have to retake its course. Think about it. How many times have you wondered, "what if…?" You know what I'm talking about. Those moments where an opportunity presented itself and you were too damn scared to just pick up a phone, email or walk through the door for fear of a potential "no," the unknown or just stepping out of your comfort zone. Or, constantly complaining about someone you work with when you know that there is nothing you can do to change neither a person nor their mind. Hey, the best thing that you can do is to alter your thoughts to change your circumstance.*

*Better yet, what about sticking in a relationship or a situation because quite frankly it became a matter of convenience and you falsely consented to the reasons why you thought you could not let go? Ladies, we've all been there! Remember agreeing to reconcile your rocky union and saying, "all is forgiven" when your spirit warned you "that you're headed for another heartbreak." But, it was the promise that "this time will be different" that got your heart quieting your head. And what about repeating the cycle of getting involved with the same type of man only to end up frustrated with sleepless nights? Yet, perhaps the most heart-wrenching one of all is as you gaze at him after a particularly heated conversation that ultimately leads to what he wants or where he stands, you silently question "if I fulfill your needs, will you up and leave me?"*

*Complicated right? Not really and certainly no more than we make it. The often neglected truth is knowledge is power and we do have it. So, if this is our reality, when will we be stronger and wiser and exercise that muscle? Bear in mind, life is already a trip girl! But how we choose to walk the path doesn't have to be.*

*Not this time will I…*

*…stop believing in me.*
*…allow my issues to get the best of me.*
*…let any words, people or*
*obstacles steal my happiness.*
*…fear anything.*
*…let anyone test me.*
*…lose sleep over someone or something.*
*…allow my emotions to cloud*
*my ability to reason.*
*…expect more and demand less.*
*…lose myself in order to have him.*
*…assume anything.*
*…allow the image of another*
*woman undermine my beauty.*
*…overlook what pleases me.*
*…stop smiling.*
*…ever forget that I am a* **Hot Chick***!*

# Nothing stops my hotness!

Beauties, now that you're feeling hot and empowered, reign over your belief with a wink and a smile because you are that **Hot Chick**, 365 days of the year - and nothing…I mean nothing…ends, disrupts or changes that…not even a man, woman, child, job, weight, lack of funds, pimple, bad hair day, stress, an evil low self-esteem moment, whatever! Remember, you are as you think you are…always. So, take a deep breath, slip on your confidence and step into your hotness one pretty thought at a time!

By the way, let's keep the *Hot Chick* movement going, shall we?! Write your own pretty thoughts on the next few pages and/or submit them online at www.prettythoughtsofahotchick.com and refer to them as often as possible to keep your hot self sizzling! And please share with your girls. We have to stick together and not only help ourselves but lend a hand to our sister **Hot Chicks** and lift each other up. The time is now.

Smile. Laugh. Live. Love.

Believe in your power!

Ciao.

**Insert your name here:**

**The Pretty Thoughts of a Hot Chick!**

_____

_____

_____

_____

_____

_____

_____

_____

_____

_____

_____

_____

_____

_____

**Insert your name here:**

**The Pretty Thoughts of a Hot Chick!**

_____

_____

_____

_____

_____

_____

_____

_____

_____

_____

_____

_____

_____

_____

**Insert your name here:**

**The Pretty Thoughts of a Hot Chick!**

_____

_____

_____

_____

_____

_____

_____

_____

_____

_____

_____

_____

_____

**Insert your name here:**

**The Pretty Thoughts of a Hot Chick!**

_____

_____

_____

_____

_____

_____

_____

_____

_____

_____

_____

_____

_____

_____

_____

_____

**Insert your name here:**

**The Pretty Thoughts of a Hot Chick!**

_____

_____

_____

_____

_____

_____

_____

_____

_____

_____

_____

_____

_____

_____

_____

**Insert your name here:**

**The Pretty Thoughts of a Hot Chick!**

_____

_____

_____

_____

_____

_____

_____

_____

_____

_____

_____

_____

_____

_____

_____

**Insert your name here:**

**The Pretty Thoughts of a Hot Chick!**

_____

_____

_____

_____

_____

_____

_____

_____

_____

_____

_____

_____

_____

**Insert your name here:**

**The Pretty Thoughts of a Hot Chick!**

_____

_____

_____

_____

_____

_____

_____

_____

_____

_____

_____

_____

_____

*H: Heavenly*

*O: Obliging*

*T: Tantalizing*

*C: Clever*

*H: Hot*

*I: Interesting*

*C: Charming*

*K: Knock-out*

# Acknowledgments

I'd like to first thank God for all of my blessings and giving me the strength to do what I do!

To my grandmother, Jessie. . .my guardian angel. . .your spirit has been my soul's greatest comfort!

To my mom Gloria, for her unyielding encouragement and unconditional love…I love you mommy! You are a beautiful woman.

To my brother Shawn and my sister Shayla, you mean the world to me…I love you both so much and I am so proud to have you cuties in my life!

To my cousins: Erica, your beauty has no boundaries just like your love; Jermaine, no one touches my mind and soul like you do!; Teshuna. . .you're a princess, baby… yesterday, today and always;  Regina, Your smile could light up a room "Re-Re"; Eric. . .one of the sweetest men I know. Vernell, you were the original fun, sexy chick and after all these years, I can still hear you laughing.

To my uncles Marvin, Clarence, Herman and Willie, the "fathers" I never had. Thank you. I love you!

To my aunts Patricia (Pat), Barbara, Judy, Grace and Ilene who taught me that a smile, laughter and charm are the tools every hot chick should have in her beauty arsenal!

To my grandfather Herman…I love you.

To Loretta, you stepped into a role that I'm sure was not easy…Thank you.

To Harvey, I forgive you daddy…finally.

To Joyce, Derrick and Sean, thank you for seeing in me what I've come too recognize and become!

To Audrey. . .your wisdom, love and grace. . .I'll treasure forever. I love you.

To Ellis, a very good man.

To Margie, thank you for always having my back girl! Your "shoulder" has been a safe heaven for me. I love you!

To Noni. . .my life has been enriched by your laughter, love and friendship.

To Christine, your terrific humor got me through some of the toughest times girlfriend!

To Pansy, true friendships never die…I love you silly bee!

To Nova, you will always be a star.

To Randy for his extraordinary talent, love, support and introducing a girl into womanhood. You are a treasure! Thank you for everything handsome! I'll always love you.

To Chad Chadwick, thank you for your kindness & support!

To Yungran Pahk, thank you for helping me sparkle!

To my baby, JOLIE Magazine, I love you so much and I gave up a lot for you…but now its time for "mommy" to have a life.

To my JOLIE readers, thank you for your love and support! You've touched me in so many ways!

To Rachel and Scott…we've not always seen eye-to-eye, but I truly appreciated your efforts. Thank you for the journey and motivating me to see what was already in me. I'll always love you for it!

To actress & producer Vivica A. Fox, for showing me the truth with glamour and tough love.

To Michelle Pascal, thank you for helping me see the light. You are one cool chick!

To Lloyd Strayhorn…my dear friend and one of the few people who "gets" me. Thank you for your love and support. I love you honey!

To Reggie, who guides me to see beyond the words, believes in me, challenges me and inspires me to be the best that I can be. Thank you so much! I love you.

To my extended family and friends, you are not forgotten!


And to all of the Hot Chicks everywhere, now and forever…continue to believe in your power and keep blazing your trail! Cheers & Live Pretty!

# bio

Alicia Marie Rivers, a twelve-year veteran of the magazine publishing industry and a budding web and TV personality, is a self-esteem and sex appeal specialist and the founder of www.jolie-magazine.com. She has held several positions within the media world. Most notably, she was the first Black female Editor-In-Chief of two non-ethnic hair & beauty magazines...*101 Hairstyles & Shortcuts*. Alicia has also successfully spearheaded the significant success of several hair, beauty, fashion and celebrity magazines including *Hot Hair*, *Ultimate Hair*, *Great Hair Now* and *Be Stylish*, *Teen Celebrity*, *Sweet 16.com*, *Celebrity Cuts*, *Black Hairstyles & Trends*, *Black Hair & Braids*, *Black Elegance* and *Belle* (a publication geared to the full-figured woman). Her talents have been featured on highly watched television programs such as **ABC News, CBS 2 News, The Montel Williams Show, The Tyra Banks Show, BET, The Jimmy Kimmel Show** and **Good Day New York**. Alicia attended Northwood Institute in Midland, MI as well as The Fashion Institute of Technology in New York City.

The Michigan native resides in New York City.